Look

Look

Look

Look
Look
Look

poems

Callista
Buchen

Black
Lawrence
Press

www.blacklawrence.com

Executive Editor: Diane Goettel
Cover Design: Zoe Norvel
Cover Art: "Midsagittal Female" by Lisa Nilsson
Book Design: Amy Freels

Published 2019 by Black Lawrence Press.
Printed in the United States.

For caregivers and those who nurture them,

with special appreciation for Mary Jo and James Kearney

CONTENTS

I

MEMORY AS FLIGHT

Here are the wings we imagine, women, printed in blood, muscle. Lush, our wish for what beats to transform rather than diminish. We say memory is not a ghost but a cityscape. Maybe it rains, maybe it even floods, feathers everywhere. The ground too soft, we map the whole town from above.

We require distance. *The rebuilding effort,* they say, *it takes time.* We lilt, we turn, we don't wait for the weather. Here we are, woman: so red no one can see us, our low moans, our bellows, beyond these bodies, these machines. Peace. We could be burned, burning, what is sacrificed. We decide to go: ash and all, our shadows too fast for the broken city below.

FLASHES

A lantern, just in case.

Mother, mother, mother, mother, mother.

Huddled in the basement. A nest of blankets under the table saw.

Needle up, down, pull through. Knot.

Sirens startle the finches roosting on the light fixture by the front door.

Clouds made of mouths.

Mother, mother, mother, mother, mother.

The needle of the compass flickers, the world made of lines and pulls.

I unravel until I am floating, dragging cords, like bleeding.

After all, they did the best they could.

Sirens, check. Radio, check. The childhood dog comes down, too.

You pick at what frays.

AFTER

She was born, when time had stretched like a muscle, contracted and hung, contracted and hung, a muscle *there in the air*, I saw I had lost my voice, bled it out, let it fall, held its strange small hand.

I can't stop saying I'm sorry. I can't stop saying oh god. Oh god.

There should've been music, or at least musicians, set up near the radiator or the bathroom door. I would've liked violins. I can picture the gleam of the polished birch, the reflection of the stain, how it wants and speaks.

I'm sorry. I had forgotten to say.

Even now, I can't remember the faces. I can't remember the women who took my voice or the blood that carried it away. There were two girls with mops. This is later, though. They said nothing.

PIECE OF ROUGH

The mother is relieved when the husband accompanies the daughter for the bath, when they take the daughter away to check and recheck her weight. In the room, the daughter's body is a balloon, body divided. The daughter needs all the air. The mother tells no one.

The mother's body pushes toward some other shape, squeezing the loss, diamond-like, until the emptiness can be cut. The mother sets an alarm to remember to feed the daughter, another to look for more air. The mother stops speaking, tries to inhale less.

All slender bruise, the daughter turns yellow. The husband changes her diapers, learns to swaddle her body in the receiving blankets. She yellows. The heel pricks begin. The husband goes with her, holds her slip of a body as she meows. In the empty room, the mother keeps her hands on her belly, tries to touch the daughter through the skin.

REGENERATION

Woman: be permeable, be ocean, be habitat. Instead of woman, say starfish. Find a tide pool. New limbs in place of those you've lost. (As if misplaced, as if not dead, as if not plucked from your body, as if not woman.) Crawl away with what remains, sink, scale, absorb each place. Woman, cover your arms in starfish, wear them across your chest, latched into your hair, be invisible, be sea. Let the salt crack across your skin. Cradle the water, what flows in and back, watch for reflexes. *There will be enough love, enough everything,* they say in support group, *there will be enough,* but woman, woman, keep track of your arms.

MANTRA

Before birth, twice the body. Doubled blood volume. *Your body is not your own*, the women laugh. Later, in the hospital basement, women sit in a circle, nursing. They could be knitting, could be planning a war. Pink-purple mouths at their breasts. The latch, the drain. What you keep alive. They could recite, *your body is not your own*, but everyone already knows. They could chant, but who has the time. The bloodletting. Cream drips onto the floor. The extra plasma and the hearts returned to rhythm, and the women, like normal, double-mouthed and thirsty.

ETHER

You have a sleeping child wrapped to your chest, your belly and hips numb, arms full, and you think, *what burns? what sails?* Let's say you are a mother.

Let's say you want to build a paddle wheel to dance inside. You think, *Why not?* You would thrash and throw your hair, how you would churn your bodies into white foam. So much of a mother is liquid.

Let's say *fog*. Even in your imagination, the wheel whirls where it stands, and you gasp, the child gasps, until the wetness slides over you like a blanket. Where do you need to go, anyway? Let's say you don't notice.

EMERGED

I see you, I touch you, I breathe onto your face, flutter. A sunken kingdom, this grounding in proximity. The elegance of *in person*, of presence. We don't distinguish between this version and that, before and after. The duplicates stand around, and the originals —no, unimportant, indistinguishable. We try to behave like human beings. We sit in a circle, let our body become the torch, dry out the old rooms, find the old habits, brush along the floors and gather debris. We breathe the dust in and breathe it out. We are civilized people. You see me, you touch me, flicker. Something buried washed away. In the rubble, you find a mirror where you can confront your double—you don't recognize her, and I'm not looking, my hands buried in the still-wet clay, making more bodies. Floods recede, broken branches, piles of bleached bricks in the shape of hotels. An old man on a bicycle. You seem taller in person. Smaller. You and I and you and I go looking for the water line, for the stain on the wall that divides eras, for the wash away and merge, for the mother who let it rain. We find an inexplicable chair, a plastic bowl, our arms and our eyes, all the things she couldn't stop.

THE VAULT

About the faulty air conditioner, about the freezer door that won't close, about the cold that won't stay put. She has to live in the world. Energy, frequency, vibration. Woman, what do you want?

She reads about mines in a magazine. The turquoise pools left behind, about extraction and minerals, how to peel into the earth's crust like skin and abandon the gash. *You can look*, the voices say. *But all the jewels have been harvested, set in another crown.* They say, *delicate, hidden.* When building means taking away, to strip.

Her milk drips on, pearl after pearl. She is not a disease. She gives over to the daughter the way the daughter finally gives over to sleep. She calls out for the body that has gone missing, for what has been carved away. Rattle, woman. Make the noise.

RECLAIMED

Woman: you are decision. The prism hanging in the windowsill, the bounce between said and imagined. Say, *refraction*—say, *desire*. So many eyes. You speak, you silence, and the specter, the voice saying, *Calm down, woman*. This, you think, could be the language of mothers. *It is universal*, they say. *It happens to everyone*. All the symmetry, as if before and after are equal.

II

METAPHYSICS

Our most ambitious work: mother as birthplace, where woman
  becomes location.
Someone singing: rejoice! A body in service, a graft here, a
  graft there.
Call and response: how she (nearly) disappears inside ritual
  and imprint.

Let's situate: Where were you born?
In a (nearly) different life, the child stands between her
  parents: a record, a stain, a photograph of the future.
Contextualize: There, says the child, pointing toward her
  mother, *home*.

Later, how (nearly) altered: child becomes mother, the X on a
  map.
Call and response: why didn't you warn me?
A prayer: but who would believe it? says the mother, and turns
  on the music.

FLASHES

Bring me to the hills.

You learn to think in breath.

I have been looking. I have been digging. I have been carrying stones.

My greatness is something like a riverbed.

Other lungs exhale questions.

It isn't fair, the way I'm saying it.

I don't see the mountain even when I'm bent, fingers in the brush.

Where are the buckets? Where is the well? Who has lifted the rain?

I'm saying it.

You must stop counting the noises. There isn't enough soap.

When it gets loud, crawl away behind your skin. Leave your face.

Cheat.

Pull back the curtain each time you hear a car. Check.

All the hills amount to burial mounds.

In. Out. Gasp. Wisp. Air, air, air.

I am the grounding.

A commercial about a movie: men take the children from a school bus and bury them alive.

Say it.

God, is she breathing. Go check to see if she is breathing. Is she breathing.

My hands hold the hills.

There is always another layer of skin.

You will have to gather them first, run from the door, through the yard.

An article about a man and a chainsaw: *By then, she had joined her husband in death.*

I need a tighter stitch, a tighter sieve.

The exhale of a fist.

Just a long line of rocks and sand.

The hands of my mother, the hands of my father.

How will you get everyone out. Say.

Quickly.

You can't get away from the knuckles.

ANOTHER

This is how another baby. The house has six rooms: this is how I wear down the carpet, bruise my foot on the broken title, how I keep my unmarked baby alive. This is how I destroy myself, how I fall on the bed, how she suckles to sleep, how each night, each feeding, how I destroy myself against myself, how I absent the six rooms, from the voices outside. *Mother, woman.* How to unfix, surrender to momentum, how the baby that grows, who needs. How to fall. This wailing. How to hold up six rooms, how to carry the babies. This is how another mother. How the curtains don't open, how the laundry becomes clean, how the blood swirls toward the shower drain. How milk ruins the pillows, mildews the mattress. Mothers. How another. How head shake. How to destroy. This is how the ghosts hold hands, how a mother calls, how to join, be process. How another house, another body, how to build. Remade, this is how.

ROAD CONSTRUCTION

A woman has commandeered all the traffic cones. No one knows where to drive, how to maneuver through holes where the intersection used to be. She keeps them in the basement and in her attic, stares at the reflective strips lining her bookshelves, until she memorizes the hazards. She wants a new rocking chair. Less celebration than so much rubber or plastic, she calls out to the horns: *I am all for the music*, and turns her arms into cradles.

LOSS

We do the research. We hear the quiet, see the heart slow, vanish. For a while, we are made of words, of *embryo*, of *viable*, of *wait and see*. I am grief. I am double and half. I carry the dead body, which is better than no body. I can be a coffin. That easy. I want to push back the waters, the wave of blood staining the sofa. It floods out. That easy, like someone pulling a cord. Like opening the blinds. Easy. The clots, the bags of blood and tissue. It goes fast, too fast to brace. Too fast to hold. Too fast to find a face. Everywhere, wet. That easy. Hollow now. Pounding at my chest, grasping at my ribs. Rocking, prying. Open this container: *Take*, I am saying, *Then take it all.*

KINDS OF TRUCKS

A crane lifts steel beams, hoists support into place. A cement mixer revolves. I organize the collection of hard hats in my closet, search catalogues for steel-toed boots. They say there is nothing like standing on top of the building you built. When I count my hard hats, I do not count the antagonists. A backhoe doesn't shovel. I pick up the hats like babies and swing them above my head to hear the gasp, until I must hammer away the roof. The dump truck unhinges, gravel barraging through the hole. From down the street, you can see my hard hats. People make blue-lined plans, make beams, monuments. They spread the concrete right over my new boots. Somewhere, a woman plans an arboretum, thinks, this morning I am domestic, this afternoon I am wild. She notices my collection of hard hats, wants to plant a cluster of cedars. What about the roof? *Of course*, she says, *you'll need a reflective vest. Of course*, I say, and just like that, we have an understanding.

APPARITION

The body now, the body before, the body that comes back to you again, as if you walk into the mirror, merge the vision of yourself with yourself. Touch your hands into the silver reflection: *this wetness*, you imagine, dripping in what could be mercury, shine, how you can't hold onto any light. You are nothing, you are springboard, you are not even wet.

The body now, the body before, all the bodies of the future, as if you could reach into the water and pull yourself, gasping and bloody, to the surface. As if you could cradle her arms and, dripping, sleep.

STORYTELLING

In *Blueberries for Sal*, Little Sal picks blueberries with her mother while a mother bear and cub eat their way through bushes on the other side of the mountain. The children get lost in the sunshine, in the sweet splashes of blue, until they follow the wrong mothers through the blue pages. Always the same story, the single color illustrations, me reading, my mother reading, her mother reading. What it means to be innocent. The mothers don't notice their missing children until the very end, until Little Sal and the mother bear snarl nose-to-nose, until Little Sal's mother realizes a bear cub must have a mother nearby. *And we all know what that means.* The happy ending: Little Sal canning in the kitchen, the baby bear asleep in the woods. The book closes (the daughter, each daughter, wants it again), but the mountain's shadow lingers like a grudge. Each mother begins again, holding for as long as she can.

III

REMNANTS

Each form she fills out asks for the number of pregnancies, the number of live births. Even at the optometrist's, the numbers don't match. She reminds the husband to condition the brown leather couch, to cover the blood stains, but he runs out of cream, forgets to go to the store. They pretend the marks are lemonade, olive oil, pasta sauce. She is always spilling, the first child is always sticky with peanut butter.

When the second child dies before he is born, before he had fingerprints, when he was a kidney bean or kumquat with webbed fingers, the third child becomes the second child. She pretends to have forgotten the thud and splash as she scrambled to the toilet, bleeding like a dog, the horrible, resolved decision to flush. The way, when she first heard, she felt better. How after she had nothing to hold.

The third child that is the second child, *any day now*. She smiles like people do when they say that. She thinks about the gray strings of tissue that took weeks to leave her body, the way something can die and be dead and not thought of for a long time, except how it changes the words, how you could read the future, study the tissue like tea leaves, and watch it change.

FLASHES

You think you know the right words, the right order.

The valley out the window, no smaller than my little finger.

My mother scatters dead marigolds.

Ask me about the salt, ask me about the wet tracks.

My memory is a storm.

What you incant, you incite.

I have buried the seeds.

My sweet girl. Oh, my sweet girl.

You keep your paper dolls under your bed.

Evaporate. Grow heavy. Rain. Evaporate.

I'm thinking of a number between one and a hundred.

You cry at what rips, at one-sidedness.

You plan to be your father.

Zucchini vines thread through chicken wire.

Where else would you go?

The sod-covered garden, indistinguishable except in recall.

I am swaying, I am breaking, I am scattered, reed-body, mosaic wind.

You say, *I will try again in the morning.*

Soft, swinging a pillow of mixed-up stones.

TO HIDE

She looks at me, face set, resisting the impulse to crumble. Already she knows which tears to hide, how to keep her eyes wide and press her lips together. *My daughter,* I think, kneeling before her as if she is an altar, whispering, *you are upset.* How she finally chokes against my shoulder, how she wants permission to feel. Or a place, a name for her pain and a body that pretends strength, which promises to keep her whole.

My daughter, I think later, as I sit on the lid of the toilet while her brother thrashes inside my belly, sobbing into a bath towel so they won't hear in the other room. All the broken bodies. The wet eyes of my mother, of her mother. I kneel, terrycloth in my mouth, but I don't know who is the prayer and who is the god. What am I supposed to promise? *My mother,* she is singing now, running at the door. *Where is my mother?* Illusion, for a while. I put on the body. The permission, while it lasts.

LOOK LOOK LOOK

At first, we think we need to wash the windows, but the problem is that they all have broken seals. Moisture grows between panels. *It is easy*, they say on the phone. *You just replace each window with a new one.*

Later, I read that the cells of children move through the placenta, latch on to the mother's lungs, liver, brain, her skin. The daughter's cells, the cells of the new baby, the cells of the baby that was lost. All the people of this body. A fissure leads to fog.

We squint when we try to watch the birds in the garden. The daughter doesn't care. She lifts her shirt and points to her navel and I tell her, *this is where we were attached.*

>*The knot on her belly.*

>*The knot on my belly.*

>*The knot on my mother's belly.*

After the baby comes out, she wants to know, can she have another turn. Then she's back to the window, pointing to what flies.

THE CENTER

I take the wedding picture from above the piano in the living room and hang it in a corner of the bedroom. *Before.* You have to look at it on purpose now, at the younger faces. I do not keep track of my eyes or my chin. No one peeks in on my hands. Maybe misplaced, my grandfather's father came over from Holland as a child. *After.* He married, built the homestead, the white house with a screened-in porch like a mouth full of teeth. *Before.* At night, I try to crawl inside my belly button. I hold back the creases as if they are heavy drapes, as if I am Moses or Charlton Heston and my belly button is the waters, as if I have somewhere to be. In my dreams, I lose the children. I pat the bed. I rip off the sheet. I'm cold, someone says. *After.* The center chasm that holds the flood. I look everywhere. Hands folded in their laps. A man in the shadow of the door. *Before.* In the road, dust as if the chariots have just sprinted by. The fluid thumping, my head down, and the cord that tethers. *After.* My fists punch my abdomen, feet brace through walls, until I melt into brush strokes. There, the line between making and being made, hands on all sides.

BIRTH RIGHT

When you count the apples, count the bruises separately.
Hold each in such a way, the sunrise, the layers of skin, fruit,
and seed. You eat it all raw. Make a sail from kitchen aprons
and apple cores.

My guided meditation says to stop saying "labor." Stop saying
"contractions." She says, *the words we choose shape what we believe.* Say,
"birthing time." Say, "pressure waves." *Reclaim your body*, she says.
Pain as belief, as language.

A tower of apples, a moat from the pulp, you moor your boat.
You swallow all the seeds you can. You climb. You have
nowhere else to go. Apple maggots, creamy like milk, tunnel
from fruit to fruit. Blinded by salt, you sit in the middle, let
the hollow and the worms wash out.

She says that I deserve an easy and comfortable birthing. She says
I *deserve* it.

Your daughter looks for you in a bowl of apples. She's hungry
for something sweet.

Breathe in to the slow count of four. Tongue on the teeth. Check
the jaw, the eyelids. Out for a count of eight. Empty apples, skin
collapsing as your daughter grabs. *There*, she says. *Now you feel so
good.*

LUNA

Moon-maker, moon-lover, I am ocean, salty, what licks. I am cave, what vacillates. *Mother* sounds like *mud*. *He knows nothing.* I am so dangerous.

My body cradled in my hands. The blood on my fingers, the printing between my thighs, the scaffold of the future, the trail of broken waters between the bed and the bathroom, the moon that illuminates. All the water in my hands. There isn't a dam you can build that I can't break. Charisma, chiasma, power. See what I will do.

RELEASE

I initial *here and here*, endorse the consent so I can get back to my body, as if the son cares about letters, as if paperwork can contain this wave. My body has its own permission. The nurse wants me to lie down.

I have been fully informed, the forms say. Indeed, this time, I kneel on the bed, face the wall. I growl and bear, my body yawning as the son slips out, the nurses surprised, the closest doctor pulled from the hallway arms out and still shouting, *do you intend to give birth in this position? Do you intend to give birth in this position?*

This time, I look at the placenta, I look at the stained sheets, this time I look at the baby. Even when I roll over, pull him to my chest, I am on my knees, always, these days, on my knees, the son and I signed in blood. *I have read and understand.* I cut the cord myself.

SLOW MOTION

Once the son is born, she gives up, folds into him, stops resisting what exhausts. She buries him in milk, his small neck in her hand. It seems everyone in the whole world sleeps. *My goals are modest*, says the mother. She could be alone, except she cannot. *It won't always be like this*, the women say to each other, this comfort, this grief.

TIDE POOLS

Your body that swells and retreats. Water that pushes forward and back, like you never get anywhere, except older. Singing: *daughter-moon, son-moon. What shall we wear away? What shall we build?*

You get used to the craters, the red rivers across your belly and thighs. The new body that vanishes, the new body that washes in. Your body that chants for return, chants for what will hold the shore and almost suffocate, for what dies in the sun or in a child's plastic pail.

> *Daughter-moon, son-moon*: for the sake of rhythm. *Collect, collect.* Shells and smooth stones.

> *Daughter-moon, son-moon*: in the sting of salt. Water or blood or who can tell. Pull, pull. Hold this liquid body, birth us again.

MILK DRUNK

I am pearl and shine, mirror and magic, a vine that rivers across bodies. *Swim, swim,* it whispers. I build and dissolve, droplets as bricks, cement as evaporation. I am light rain, hard rain, thunder, hail. What leaves a mark and crinkles underfoot.

We are lashed with milk. Versions float, creamed and sticky, a dilated eye. I am rope and tether and you are the kick, kick, the reach and pull (*swim away, swim away*). We could drown in what drips down my belly, in your arch and cough. You lap. I am a lake, the heat that comes, what absorbs. I turn, I spoil, I empty and dry, even forget.

IV

QUICK CHANGE

She keeps her body around the house. There is body in the coat closet in the hall by the front door, body under the bed in plastic bins, a pile in the garage by the recycling bin. The spares, she calls them. She misplaces her body like she loses her keys. She releases it, lets her body carry her from this room to that, lets her body stretch until it must be replaced. *It is better this way*, she says, slipping into a fresh one as the baby cries. *I never have to worry about being recognized*.

FLASHES

I hammer and turn, and everything I touch goes glass.

A mountain made of houses, all the walls and doors.

You don't know what to say.

My mother watches. My father watches.

Where else would you go?

Someone imagines climbing through a window.

A whole forest of parents, a brickyard of parents.

I can't, I say. I can't.

Whispers: lie down with the baby. Map the baby. Build the baby.

I find sharp edges. I make sharp edges.

You wrap up in arms.

SWADDLE

At home, the baby might as well be in a museum, under glass, his perfect fingernails, how he smells of melon and flour, wrapped and wrapped in muslin until he is preserved. This is your job now. *Look*, you could be saying to visitors, *at what has been saved! See his open mouth, how he uses all this room to breathe.* You are the alarm, the resin, the final word on keeping him alive. You document, record, and wrap him again like the artifact you imagine him to be. You do everything right and lie when you don't. *Look*, you say. *Look*.

LINEA NIGRA

This could be the poem about how the poem is a child and the child is the poem, but that would be bullshit.

The dark line down my belly doesn't go away, what wants to be a lie or at least a myth, but isn't, this place where my body split open for another body. *The poem in that,* I say to the midwife as she pokes my belly, feels the muscles that have separated, measures the distance between wrecked and whole.

What a fucking metaphor, I tell the husband later, ignoring the surgery pamphlet on the table, the picture of a man and his needle, my hands at my belly button, holding my insides together. I am this splitting, the exhausted gap. I am scar, I am pieces. The body as the poem, what won't grow back.

VOID

A mother is full of cracks, this vessel. Everywhere tears, every-where salt. What is lost. *A body collects what it holds*, thinks the mother. *I am made of space.*

The mother dams herself, gathers the body that swells and runs. For a while, everything stops: her plugged milk ducts and tear ducts, how she grows hot and hard and red-streaked, her body some other animal. She stockpiles nets and pillows, grinds bricks into sandbags, but the walls she builds are empty. Each morning, the sheets are damp.

Someday, to find what hasn't washed away, she will lower bells or cement or a small yellow bird down into the holes. She will find an apple tree, a white cloth, or a jewel, and there on the wall, the handprints of her children, the kind of thing she keeps in the closet for no reason, but can't throw away.

THE VIRTUES OF CEMENT

All the water, the constant wetness, overwhelms you. You see now that cement is the way to go. You like the way after you are gone, you won't have to watch the destruction, how someone else will jackhammer your sidewalk, your basement, your backyard slab with its initials and dates. A leftover pile of unnatural rocks. You know better.

Cement won't catch fire. Water won't hold shape. Water spreads until contained, water evaporates and seems to vanish, water seeps and seeps and seeps. How can we build from dampness? From a retreating edge? You might be burning. Cement gives you baseline, foundation, something to drill into and believe. You aren't even after permanence. Water cycles, false starts and returns. You build your wall and wait, eyes wet with smoke.

COUNTER-PRESSURE

As if this could be the poem, she thinks, pacing in the dark. The baby with pink cheeks, his teeth coming soon, how she remembers doing this before. How she keeps him close, her chin on his forehead, how she tries to be outside her body, holding him but not holding him. The lines walked one after another, the husband who promises to stay awake and falls asleep, the daughter who calls out, the mother, the body that rages, who resists forgiving. Her finger rubs the baby's broken gums. There is nothing malicious here. She walks the same lines, writes the same poem, holds their innocence like a lantern toward what she already knows.

TORNADO

I insist on a safe room, something guaranteed to stand the wind. *This is life on the prairie,* I say. The men bring bolts, drive rebar through concrete. We make everything hard. The steel room out in the garage, loaded with gallons of water, the extra pairs of shoes, the threat. I know a mother who plans to tip the dryer over her children during a storm. *What can I do,* she says, and we all nod.

The weather is easy enough. After the children are asleep, I make dinners for the week and freeze them, I refill the soap dispensers, I sort laundry, as if I can hold back the threat. I curl against the tile floor in the kitchen and stay up late making lists, drawing maps. When I mistake the wind for a woman weeping, I wake the husband. *Where can I get more steel,* I ask him, my fingers on the baby's chest, counting breaths.

SADNESS

The husband brings his sadness out to show her. *Look*, he says, *how big!* The mother hates the husband's sadness, wants to stab the sadness with the steak knives, to cut it up into little pieces and feed it to the dog, only they don't have a dog, but she would get one just to eat up his sadness.

He squints and holds it up to the light, shakes it until bits of sadness cover the mantle, sprinkle the counter, float in the daughter's cereal. They are all coughing. The mother says, *I need some air*, and picks up the shovel and goes outside to try to bury her sadness like a bone or a body. She watches the husband and the children through the window the whole time.

OF ALL THE REASONS

She knows she isn't pregnant again, that they have been careful. But, what the hell? Maybe? For the third month in a row, she watches the solitary line appear, and she cries because she is sad but not about this. What she wants is to be bulldozed into difference, to soothe a burn rather than to build a fire, to have to react. How do you go back to being a person? She is cold. She is stupid. She pries the test apart, holds the strip up to the light, just in case, and throws everything away.

ONWARD

Woman, turn your feet around.

Be asleep in your body. When you walk, act as if your arms are open windows, like your body is all mortar and brick. Woman, turn inward. Stretch into the crack.

When hands reach for your body, you cry out. They say, *smile, woman*. This time, you use all your teeth and snap. The dirt flies. You are so hungry.

CURB APPEAL

I read somewhere that having a child is a kind of death, which relieves me. A kind of permission to set my life on fire. I can tell them to stop looking. *She's already gone*, I say. An elegant disappearance: gradation rather than saturation, a flint, the turn of a kaleidoscope. I am orange or pale blue, some opposite color. Not the tone itself, but its sense, the difference between a shape and the color of that shape. We can paint the house and the sun bleaches it back. The shadow doesn't change until we knock it down.

FLASHES

I drape. I unfold. I smooth the dragging threads.

She hates falling asleep.

You practice smiling, trying to look natural.

The cedar trees eaten inside out by parasites: you don't know until it's over.

The desire to check, recheck. How you teach yourself not to leave the bed, because if you get up to check, you'll go back.

I'm sorry for yelling. I'm sorry for yelling. I'm sorry for yelling.

She walks by a carton of oranges scattered on the lawn, bright bulbs against the snow.

Every day, you are late to preschool drop off.

The daughter's greatness is a canyon, is a flood.

You can tell me anything. I want you to know, you can tell me anything.

Usually we can't see the dying.

Peel the fruit, scored with a knife, lift each piece with the back of the spoon, give each slice to a child.

You girls be quiet up there.

All this as a garden. Pith like lace.

You can tell me anything. I want you to know, you can tell me anything.

NEXT, THE EARS

In the evenings, house asleep, I try to take out my eyes and put them in a glass of water on the blue nightstand next to the bed. But another pair pops into place, not unlike the yogurt that slides down each time I take a new one out of the cooler at the grocery store where I forgot to buy eggs. I take out my eyes until the glass of water is full, the eyes at the top barely in the water, red-stained and itching. I gaze at my eyes, coolly, as if I distrust them, and then we all laugh, the way you can with your eyes. We are fluid, open like a face. Maybe we didn't even want the eggs. By the time someone starts crying, the glass of water is a glass of water, and all the eyes are back in line, pair by pair.

MAGICAL THINKING

She's not sure these days, about what can be predicted and what cannot, about the richness of other people's lives. *I'm done*, she keeps telling friends, but at night, she brainstorms lists of more children, how she likes the idea of naming. The husband sleep-walks down a hallway. She calls him back to bed. He sighs and settles. Outside, a whistle, the rumble. Another train charges by, another. Her grief is elsewhere, in what refuses naming, in what she cannot yet hold long enough to placate, in the morning that comes and comes.

FIGURE

Woman, you are the not the first.

You mistake sand for water, you blame your confusion on the sun. *Split* looks like *multiply*, *many* could almost mean *more*. You think you read the reflections, the near misses, as if you understand what you see. What births, divides. Imagine: cuttings of saffron, cuttings of holly, strawberry, sequoia, plants hundreds of yards (or is it years) apart. Your impossible body, your impossible claim.

PRETEND

For a while, my daughter worried about a catastrophic hole in the ground wherever we were going. *Mom, what if the library is just a giant hole? What if the cereal aisle is a big hole?* She imagined canyons replacing each familiar landmark. At every intersection, every turn, I promised her there would no hole. She'd plead: *But what will we do? You'll see,* I would say, *everything will be fine.* When she stopped asking, I grieved her lost worry like the death of an imaginary friend, but since she's first stacked the blocks in the living room, she's understood that what we build we can crash. *Anything can go boom,* she says now to her little brother, who wants the tower higher, higher still. *Mom will hold it,* she tells him. She pauses and adds, *for now.*

TAKING CARE

I sit with my grief. I mother it. I hold its small, hot hand. I don't say, *shhh*. I don't say, *it is okay*. I wait until it is done having feelings. Then we stand and we go wash the dishes. We crack open bedroom doors, step over the creaks, and kiss the children. We are sore from this grief, like we've returned from a run, like we are training for a marathon. *I'm with you all the way*, says my grief, whispering, and then we splash our face with water and stretch, one big shadow and one small.

THRESHOLD

How she measures the days and their small bodies against her own. The child curled against her arm, against her ribs, the toddler on her chest. Everyone is breathing. She builds her body into *home*, into *refuge*, tries to fall into the moment like a well.

Her body is a fortress. Her body is a monument. She wants to say, *but where is the original map? But where have we buried my body?* You can't ask this of children. She grows stiff, tries to hold them until she becomes a door, and they all walk through.

ACKNOWLEDGMENTS

Alice Blue Review: "Flashes" (as "Remains")

Atticus Review: "Loss"

Baltimore Review: "Tornado"

Connotation Press: An Online Artifact: "Threshold"

decomP: "Next, the Ears"

DMQ Review: "Pretend"

Fourteen Hills: "Kinds of Trucks"

Handsome: "Mantra"

Harpur Palate: "To Hide"

Indianapolis Review: "Apparition," "Swaddle"

Josephine Quarterly: "Onward"

Journal of Compressed Creative Arts: "Sadness"

Juked: "Flashes" (as "Remains)

La Vague: "Emerged," "Imposter," "Reclaimed"

Literary Mama: "After"

Mom Egg Review: "Milk Drunk," "Release"

The Offing: "Quick Change"

Paper Nautilus: "Birth Right," "Slow Motion"

Parcel: "The Center"

Political Punch: Contemporary Poems on the Politics of Identity (Sundress
    Press): "Regeneration"

Puerto del Sol: "Regeneration"

Rogue Agent: "Memory as Flight"

Salt Hill: "Remnants"

Stirring: "Ether"

TAB: "Curb Appeal"

Thrush: "Figure," "Taking Care"

Tinderbox Poetry Review: "Road Construction," "Luna"

Whiskey Island Review: "Piece of Rough," "The Vault"

Select pieces also appear in *Double-Mouthed*, a chapbook from dancing girl press.

I'm grateful to the organizations and people that made this book possible, with particular thanks to the editors of the journals where pieces from this project first found a home, and to the remarkable team at Black Lawrence Press. Thank you, also, to my teachers, administrators, colleagues, friends, and students at Bowling Green State University, the University of Kansas, and Franklin College, and to all the writers who guided and supported this project. I'm grateful for the community that bolstered me as I became a parent: to Alicia Erikson, for her sustaining friendship; to Heather Rogge, for her kindness to me and my children; to Sarah Darby, my midwife, who helped me to heal and trust; to my doulas; and to the incredible group of care-providing friends and family who facilitated the time and space for me to write this book. Finally, thank you to Noah, Audrey, and Frederick, my very favorite people.

Photo: Megan Kearney

Callista Buchen is the author of *Look Look Look* (Black Lawrence Press, 2019) and the chapbooks *Double-Mouthed* (dancing girl press, 2016) and *The Bloody Planet* (Black Lawrence Press, 2015). Her work appears in *Harpur Palate, Puerto del Sol, Fourteen Hills,* and many other journals, and she is the winner of *DIAGRAM*'s essay contest. She teaches at Franklin College in Indiana, where she directs the visiting writers reading series and advises the student literary journal.